God's Tais

Melanie Lotfali

Atesa, Akala, Aleki, Zenha and Abel love their parents. One day they decide to make a present for their parents. They go to buy some cotton to make tais.

Atesa's favorite color is green.
She makes a green tais.
Akala likes yellow.
She makes a yellow tais.

Aleki's favorite color is red.
He uses red cotton to
make a tais for his parents.
Zenha thinks that pink
is the most beautiful.

Abel says that
blue is the best.
He makes a blue tais.

When they finish their tais
the children go and play.
They leave the scraps of
cotton on the ground.
Ameta walks past and finds the
cotton left by the other children.
She uses the cotton to make a tais.

Atesa's parents like the green tais that Atesa made for them.

Akala, Aleki, Zenha and
Abel's parents also like
the yellow, red, pink and blue tais
that their children made for them.

But Ameta's parents were the happiest of all because their tais was made of many different colors.

The people of the world are
many different colors.
Different colored cotton
makes a tais more beautiful.
And different colored people make
our world family more beautiful.

Copyright © 2013 Melanie Lotfali

God's Tais
by Melanie Lotfali is licensed
under a Creative Commons
Attribution-NonCommercial-ShareAlike 4.0
International License.

ISBN 978-0-9945817-7-8